BALLAD TO AN IOWA FARMER

Ballad to an Iowa Farmer

and Other Reflections by CLARK MOLLENHOFF

Sketches by Kevin Lind and Chris Bowring

IOWA STATE UNIVERSITY PRESS / AMES

Authorization to photocopy items for internal or personal use, or the internal or personal use of specific clients, is granted by Iowa State University Press, provided that the base fee of $.10 per copy is paid directly to the Copyright Clearance Center, 27 Congress Street, Salem, MA 01970. For those organizations that have been granted a photocopy license by CCC, a separate system of payments has been arranged. The fee code for users of the Transactional Reporting Service is 0-8138-1458-8/91 $.10.

⊗ Printed on acid-free paper in the United States of America

First edition, 1991

Library of Congress Cataloging-in-Publication Data

Mollenhoff, Clark R.
  Ballad to an Iowa farmer and other reflections / by Clark Mollenhoff. — 1st ed.
    p.   cm.
  ISBN 0-8138-1458-8 (alk. paper)
  1. Farm life — Iowa — Poetry. 2. War poetry, American. I. Title.
PS3563.0414B3   1991
811′.54 — dc20   91-11279

To my grandchildren and my step-grandchildren
with love and the hope it will give them
a better understanding of the precious moments
that make up our lives.

CONTENTS

FOREWORD

by William G. Murray

Why did Ronald Reagan get such a kick out of Clark Mollenhoff's poem "Teacher" that he committed it to memory and recited it in presenting the Teacher award of the year at the White House in 1987? Why did Meredith Willson call Mollenhoff's poem "Music Man" a smash hit? And why did I find in his "Ballad to an Iowa Farmer" a remarkable poet's interpretation of the 1900 farm at Living History Farms near Des Moines?

The answer to these questions is the key to this unique collection of poems. The author starts off with a prologue describing his lifelong love for poetry and inability to keep from writing verse. Mollenhoff wore two hats—as investigative reporter and poet—and wore both of them well. In this book he gives us not only a revealing prologue but also a description of the situation that inspired each poem. Thus we have a marvelous background to enhance personal enjoyment of each poem and even to help us pick a favorite poem.

Now to answer why Reagan, Willson, and I were especially attracted to certain poems—*our* favorites. In the Prologue Mollenhoff tells about the large number of letters of appreciation he received from farmers and former farmers after the publication of "The Old Workhorse." Mollenhoff says, "I had touched a nostalgic chord." And so he had—and for Ronald Reagan, Meredith Willson, and Bill Murray, as well.

You who are about to read this book should find at least one poem where Mollenhoff strikes a responsive nostalgic chord. You should not find it difficult. One of the features of this book is the variety of topics the author has chosen for his poems. Although the book begins with farming, a look at the Table of Contents reveals a wide choice, with many depicting different situations the author experienced in World War II.

My favorite, "Ballad to an Iowa Farmer," is a natural for me. I spent my boyhood summers working on a farm, spent forty-five years teaching farm economics, and spent another twenty-five years (eight of them while teaching) working on Living History Farms. When I saw these lines,

> His faith in God
> And Iowa sod,
> In summer rains and sun —

I felt how truthfully Mollenhoff portrayed his grandfather and how we had worked so hard to portray that farmer in the 1900 farm.

Then this timeless part touched my nostalgic chord:

> When neighbors helped
> Farm neighbors out,
> As farm folks often do,

It happens when there is sickness, an accident, or death, and it's as true today as it was in 1900. Farmers take big risks when putting their land, labor, seed, and machinery into planting, tending, and harvesting their crops — not knowing ahead of time what their crops will yield or what price they will get. It's no wonder that when adversity hits the farm family, neighbors help.

In closing, let me once again urge *you* to pick a favorite.

PROLOGUE

In William Wordsworth's preface to "Lyrical Ballads," the Lake Country poet explained his view of what poetry is and what it should be. The man who was later to be England's poet laureate said, "Poetry is the most philosophic of all writing . . . its object is truth . . . carried alive into the heart by passion." Wordsworth further explained that in his view poetry is "the spontaneous overflow of powerful feelings: it takes its origin from emotion recollected in tranquility." I agree with Wordsworth's definition. As a reporter and author I have chronicled events over a half century, with an emphasis on accuracy and truth and always with an effort to keep my emotions out of my writings. For me, the poet, too, must first of all be accurate in the word sketch being drawn and must be a clear communicator of his or her own emotional reaction. If the facts are flawed or if the report of that reaction does not ring true, it will be apparent to perceptive readers.

Many people who know of me as an investigative reporter and author have been surprised when they read my poetry, having gained the impression that I was unfeeling or that I had somehow over the years killed my natural emotions. It is true that good, effective investigative reporting requires the reporter to keep personal feelings out of the investigation and out of the finished story, to rely upon well-documented facts and highly credible sources to make the point in a manner, as near as possible, devoid of emotion.

But my avid and persistent pursuit of stories involving corruption in government, labor, or business has always been fueled by a deep personal desire to see wrongs righted and truth prevail, often a long and tedious process requiring deep faith.

My interest in poetry, in fact, predates my interest in investigative reporting. Over the years, poetry has been my avocation, a pleasurable diversion from the disciplined course of objective investigative reporting. Yet, I've found it to demand the same kind of discipline as a carefully worded lead in a news story. As in the news story lead, poetry demands brevity, precise accuracy, and color, within the framework of propriety and truth. From a mechanical standpoint it requires the same trying, and striking out, of words with slightly different shades of meaning until I am satisfied that I have finally found the word that says precisely what I want it to say.

To me, good poetry is not the result of scribbling down the first words that flash to mind. Although hasty notes may be a starting point, the finished product is a result of writing and rewriting to create the precise rhythm and/or rhyme that fits the mood and message the poet is trying to communicate. Although poetry may involve either rhythm or rhyme (or neither) I have found that—up to this time—*both* suit my purpose. This requires discipline and research, and the reading aloud of the poem to others to test the flow of words.

Poetry should be like painting—catching an emotional scene in words so natural and well chosen that they strike a deep chord of empathy in all who read them.

I cannot remember when my interest in and love of poetry started, nor can I remember when I made my first effort to write in verse. Nursery rhymes recited by my mother gave me my first interest in rhythms and rhymes, and my father's songs, both popular and spiritual, and his bass ballads provided still another association.

At St. Joseph's Catholic School in Lohrville, Iowa, I recall seeing Jean-François Millet's painting of a French peasant and reading Edwin Markham's poem, "The Man with the Hoe," inspired by the painting. At about that same time, leafing through one of the volumes of the Modern Library at home, I came across two lines of verse below a picture of an older man, a grandfatherly figure, and a small boy with a skull in his hands. The cutline carried only this verse from Robert Southey's poem, "The Battle of Blenheim":

> " 'Tis some poor fellow's skull," said he,
> "Who fell in the great victory."

I read those words over until I could repeat them from memory, impressed with the brief but eloquent message on the price of war.

At Lohrville Consolidated School in the eighth, ninth, and tenth grades, I was involved in singing in the glee club, in a boys' quartet, and in baritone solo work. The poetry of William Shakespeare, Julia Ward Howe, Francis Scott Key, Katherine Lee Bales, and Joyce Kilmer that I sang made a deep impression upon me. I found it a great pleasure to repeat the moving words.

My introduction to the poetry of Rudyard Kipling was through Miss Doreen Cobb, the voice teacher at Lohrville High School. When I was a freshman she selected me to be the baritone soloist for the school and my solo was "The Road to Mandalay," with words by Kipling and music by Oley Speaks. I became a Kipling fan and can still recite the words from that poem.

Miss Cobb introduced me to many other songs with beautiful and inspirational poetry, such as "Invictus." The poem was written by William Ernest Henley, the music by Bruno Huhn. First published in 1910, it was a standard work for baritone and bass soloists in the early 1930s. Those words I learned over fifty years ago have been a comfort when I have been faced with serious problems or doubt about my ability to stand up to a challenge. The final verse was particularly inspirational:

> It matters not how straight the gate,
> How charged with punishment the scroll,
> I am the master of my fate,
> I am the captain of my soul.

"Prayer Perfect," by James Whitcomb Riley, was another song-poem that fascinated and enchanted me with its simplicity, as did Joyce Kilmer's "Trees," set to music by Oscar Rasbach. I was fascinated with patriotic poetry from World War I, such as Alan Seeger's moving "I Have a Rendezvous with Death." Seeger's death a short time after writing the poem makes the words particularly compelling. The rollicking ballads of life in India by Kipling and those of Robert Service on the Alaskan mining camps enthralled me, as did the mystic and morbid poems of Edgar Allan Poe.

Long ago I memorized Thomas Gray's "Elegy in a Country Church Yard," and I still recall some of the verses because of the ageless appeal to anyone who has been on a cattle farm.

> The curfew tolls the knell of parting day,
> The lowing herd winds slowly o'er the lea,
> The ploughman homeward plods his weary way,
> And leaves the world to darkness and to me.

That verse jumps to mind on any late afternoon or evening when I see cattle walking down a lane or across a pasture. I envy Gray's ability to catch such a clear picture with a universal theme.

In my high school years, I became obsessed with a desire to write poetry that would catch a mood or a scene of someone's portrait with the timeless appeal of the poems I admired. I do not recall when I first tried to write verse, but I was making a few efforts by the time I was in Miss Fern Denman's eighth-grade English class. I wrote romantic verse and humorous (as I viewed them) limericks. Good, bad, or indifferent, the verses did win some laudatory comments from the young ladies in the class, and my recitation of poetry caught the attention of a ninth-grade English teacher, J. Burton Flesner, who recruited me to do dramatic readings in high school competition. I enjoyed learning how to pronounce difficult words, and to read with a rhythm that made each thought clear.

During this same period, I became involved in vocal groups, voice lessons, and baritone solo work under the enthusiastic and confidence-building tutoring of Miss Cobb.

The music in the voice classes included "Who Is Sylvia," set to words by William Shakespeare; "The Rosary," by Robert Cameron Rogers; "Believe Me, If All Those Endearing Young Charms," by Thomas Moore; "The Lost Chord," by Adelaide Anne Procter; "America the Beautiful," by Katherine Lee Bates; "A Perfect Day," by Carrie Jacobs-Bond; "Rocked in the Cradle of the Deep," by Emma Willard; and "The Star-Spangled Banner," by Francis Scott Key. All were popular traditional works of the era.

My father's transfer to Algona took me from the intellectually stimulating environment of Lohrville High School. My interest in music and poetry continued, but not my obsession with singing and with writing verse. Without Miss Cobb's enthusiastic prodding, I became more involved with athletics — basketball and baseball at St. Cecelia's Academy at Algona and football, basketball, and track at Lincoln High School in Webster City. My interest in writing was kept alive, although on a back burner, in English literature and journalism classes with Miss Ethel Swanson. She insisted on our memorizing passages and poetry from Shakespeare and other English writers, but I was too much involved with athletics to do any serious creative writing.

When we moved to Webster City in the summer of 1937, novelist and native son MacKinlay Kantor was the local hero. His book, *The Voice of Bugle Ann,* had been made into a popular movie, and he was in Webster City for a few weeks to do research on a novel dealing with Indian history in north central Iowa. It was exciting to study under the same teachers who had taught Kantor only seventeen years earlier and to read his novels, which were a focus of special attention at the Kendall Young Library. Kantor lore led to my later adoption of him as a role model.

Poetry and music again became a major focus when I entered Miss Cecelia Rudin's freshman English class at Webster City Junior College. Miss Rudin not only reawakened my interest in poetry, but she introduced me to *The Autobiography of Lincoln Steffens* and the work of the great muckraking reporters of the turn of the century. Reading about Steffens, a great investigative reporter, stirred my interest in ferreting out corruption and mismanagement in government. Steffens also had a deep interest in art, poetry, and music.

Steffens's thesis that there is always opportunity for better work in every field helped me build my confidence and develop an optimistic outlook. At the age of nineteen, with only limited experience on the school newspaper and writing sports for the *Webster City Observer,* I applied for, and landed, a reporting job on the *Des Moines Register.* I was about to be graduated from Webster City Junior College and had a football scholarship at Drake University in Des Moines.

As a cub reporter on the *Register* staff, I saw reporters laboring over the lead paragraphs of news and feature stories, rewriting dozens of times in an effort to present the precise facts and mood. The aim was to achieve an accurate and maybe poetic lead in a hundred words or less. Most of my early stories were routine police and court reports, but I had an occasional opportunity to be creative. However, most of my efforts at poetic leads were disasters. I longed for the day when I would be able to write leads like Louis Cook, Jr., George Mills, Lula Mae Coe, Dick Spry, George Shane, Elise Shane, or Florence Swihart. I saw that memorable leads did not come easily, and that even Louey Cook, the most natural poet of the lot, would labor for hours on that first important sentence or two.

With hesitation, I approached Louey Cook to show him my poetry. He was only a few years older than I but was one of my heroes, already a star reporter whose writing was admired by the entire newsroom staff. Louey found some merit in the poems and pointed out a few couplets he believed to be excellent and imaginative. He thought much of my verse was overwritten, however, and said I used extravagant words, which he termed "purple prose," when simpler ones would have better fit the mood. "It will strike a false note with the reader if it is overwritten," Louey advised. "Be a good reporter of the facts and your own emotions and you will be a good poet." I never forgot his advice, and that a star reporter had taken the time to read the fumbling poetic efforts of an inexperienced cub reporter and had given him encouragement.

Also helpful at the time were the constructive suggestions and approval of Jeannette Eyerly, the wife of *Register* Managing Editor Frank Eyerly. In addition to working as a police and court reporter for the *Register,* I was the Eyerlys' yard man—mowing their lawn, trimming the bushes, and helping Jeannette with her planting and weeding. She wrote children's books and had an enthusiastic interest in poetry. Jeanette expressed surprise when she learned of my interest and read my poetry with quiet approval and with a few excellent suggestions for the change of a word or a phrase.

All of this led to the public exposure of one of my poetic efforts on radio station WHO, Des Moines, during World War II. Len Howe, a versatile announcer and news reader, had an evening poetry program either just before or after the late news—I don't recall whether I sent the poem "Tommy" to him or whether someone else took the initiative. It was written in reaction to the death of Army Air Corps Lieutenant Thomas Kohlhaas, of Algona, Iowa. Tommy was the younger brother of John Kohlhaas, who tagged along as John and I played basketball and baseball or roamed the streets in Algona. His death was one of the first of anyone I had known well.

"Tommy" was popular with Len Howe, and with at least some segment of his listening audience. He played it countless times in response to requests from his fans. It was a big morale booster for me and encouraged me to write dozens of new poems.

Later, when I was in the Navy in World War II, I found the quiet solitude of an officer's stateroom on an attack transport provided a near ideal environment for the composition of poetry. My writing was impelled by the experience of being away from my wife and children and by observing the life of the sailors in the crew and the Army and Marine troops we carried to combat areas in New Guinea, the Philippines, and Japan. Some of the poems dealt with my experiences as a farmhand on an Iowa farm—shocking oats, pitching bundles on a threshing run, plowing corn, and working with the farm livestock. While recognizing downright drudgery of much farm work, I remembered the compensations of freedom and of the sense of accomplishment in producing something of value.

When I was discharged from the Navy in 1946, I joined the Iowa Poetry Day Association, made up of aspiring poets of all ages from all over the state. Paul Engle, already a poet of some stature, spoke before one of our meetings in Des Moines. In his talk he spoke of the importance of the little things that make up the big picture we were trying to paint with words.

Within a few months of Engle's speech I had an opportunity to follow his suggestion on a visit to the farm my grandfather, Jim Clark, had owned and farmed near Lohrville. I walked down to the barn where I had spent many delightful hours as a boy, where I had learned to milk cows and feed and harness the horses. Inside the barn there were no horses and no cattle. The main stall boards had been removed, and pigs grunted in the dirty place where the clean and strong work horses had been housed three decades earlier. To me it was almost sacrilegious for pigs to live in the stalls where my grandfather's beautiful Belgian horses had stood. There were still some horsehairs wedged in the wooden stall posts, an old and battered currycomb was on a shelf, and an old bit and remnants of harness remained of the time I had known and loved.

On the road to town, I looked for horses in the fields or around the barns. There were none for more than two miles, where there had been dozens in the 1920s and 1930s. The old teams of horses that I saw were past their prime, probably kept around for sentimental reasons. Within a few days those little things I had observed became part of "The Old Work-horse":

> A currycomb, an old check rein,
> The curb bit for the bay —
> The farm horse ghosts still linger there,
> In shadows bare and gray.

That first verse remained pretty much the same, but the other verses were rewritten and revised a number of times before the entire poem was published in the *Sunday Register*'s

"Picture Magazine" in March of 1957 and a few weeks later in the *Minneapolis Sunday Tribune*'s "Picture Magazine." Subsequently, it was reprinted by a number of farm publications with accompanying pictures of harnessed workhorses pulling wagons, plows, hay rakes, and hayracks.

Letters came from all over the Middle West from farmers and former farmers. I had touched a nostalgic chord, and they had appreciated it. Those letters pleased me as much, and perhaps more, than many of the accolades I received for my investigative reporting.

Two of my poems, "Teacher" and "Music Man," have had particularly interesting histories. In the late 1940s or early 1950s, I was thinking about the teachers in various schools in Iowa who had inspired me in many ways. Teachers are the gods of the young, I mused, because they often are responsible for the molding — or the shattering — of dreams of their students. My mother was my first teacher, and later teachers kept my dreams and others' dreams alive.

From that background came the first lines of "Teacher":

> You are the molders of their dreams —
> The gods who build or crush their young
>   beliefs in right and wrong.
> You are the spark that sets aflame a poet's hand,
> Or lights the flame in some great singer's song.

Those lines remained unchanged from the first time I wrote them, but others were revised many times in the several years I used the poem in parent and teacher forums. Later, it was published in the *Sunday Register*'s "Picture Magazine" in May 1957, along with a picture of the Iowa Teacher of the Year, on the same weekend that Ronald Reagan, then a movie star with Iowa roots, was serving as Grand Marshal of the Veishea Parade, part of the spring festival at Iowa State University. "Teacher" was an immediate hit with Iowa teachers' organizations and appeared in a number of educational publications. Apparently, Ronald Reagan had noticed the poem, because he began to use it in speeches before educational organizations.

Many years later, in the summer of 1982, I received a call

from the White House from a researcher inquiring if I was the author of "Teacher." President Reagan wanted to use the poem as a closer in a speech before a national Parent-Teacher Association meeting in Albuquerque, New Mexico. After writing the poem from memory, the president had sent the handwritten copy of the poem to his speech writers, who were checking to be certain it was precisely right.

President Reagan used my poem many times afterward, including the ceremony in the East Room of the White House before the group of finalists in the Teacher in Space program. Christa McAuliffe requested signed copies for herself and the other nine finalists. She told me she planned to take a copy with her on the subsequently tragic space launch in 1986.

President Reagan made it a matter of routine to give handwritten copies of "Teacher" to the National Teacher of the Year. He also gave a handwritten copy to Secretary of Education William Bennett, who hung it on the wall of his office. At the White House ceremony for Guy Doud, the Brainerd, Minnesota, high school teacher honored as Teacher of the Year for 1987, President Reagan recited the poem. He then wrote out from memory a version of the poem for Doud. Months later Doud recited "Teacher" beautifully and meaningfully on a thirty-minute video, "Molders of Dreams," produced and distributed by the organization Focus on the Family. It resulted in requests for signed copies of "Teacher" from teachers all over the United States and Canada.

After the publication of "Teacher," I again followed the advice of Paul Engle when writing a poem called "Music Man." This poem was inspired by my younger brother, Clair Mollenhoff, who for twenty years was a band director at a number of schools in northeast Iowa. Clair was in his first years of teaching music at the small town of Edgewood, Iowa, when I visited one of his school's practice sessions. I had tried to play a bass horn with the Lohrville school band but dropped out after a few disastrous concerts. In those few weeks, I had become familiar with practice sessions in the high school gymnasium and the raucous sound of band members tuning their instruments. I still had a secret yearning to achieve some dexterity on a musical instrument.

Clair was intense when he rapped to bring the tuning session to a close and to bring the band together in some semblance of harmony. It was a picture that remained etched in my memory. I scratched out the first words of the poem:

> His face seemed stern, but warmness
> filled his voice.
> It seemed to stretch to greet the
> youngsters there.
> His eyes were quick in measuring each
> choice
> Of woodwind, brass horn, string, bass
> drum, or snare.

This pattern of rhyme and rhythm eventually wove itself into "Music Man."

I wrote and rewrote it countless times before giving a copy to Iowan Meredith Willson, creator of the famous musical, *Music Man,* at a Washington cocktail party where he was the guest of honor. I talked with him only briefly and handed him the folded poem, suggesting that he might find time to read it later. He shoved it in a side pocket, and I didn't expect to hear from him again. Several days later I received a call from Meredith from Los Angeles. He praised me for catching the school band scene as he remembered it, suggested a change of one or two words in one verse — which I quickly accepted — and said he hoped to use the poem with my permission. I was elated that a man who wrote most of the words as well as the music for a successful musical would make such favorable comments.

A few months later, I received a letter from Meredith requesting permission to use "Music Man" in a speech at the University of Michigan. Afterward, he wrote to me on January 19, 1971:

Dear Clark:

I can't begin to tell you what a smash hit your "Music Man" poem was at the Dr. William Revelli Retirement Dinner at the University of Michigan in Ann Arbor last Friday. The poem would be great under any circumstances at any affair. However, on such an occasion, delivered to an audience of three hundred or more guests, all of whom are professional music educators, the warmth of the reaction was indescribable.

I was surprised and gratified that "Music Man" had been so well received by Meredith and that forum.

Of the millions of words that I have written in a career that has stretched over fifty years, none have given me more pleasure than my poetry and the knowledge that lines I wrote twenty, thirty, or forty years ago strike a chord with men and women I do not know and may never meet. While I have found satisfaction in righting a few wrongs along the way, few moments can compare with the thrill of hearing Meredith Willson express admiration for my "Music Man."

There has also been pleasure in the calls and letters from individual teachers and the requests from teachers' organizations to distribute "Teacher" in both small and large school systems. Likewise, there has been deep satisfaction in calls and letters from old and young farmers about "The Old Workhorse" and other farm poems.

Wilfred A. (Bill) Groves, a longtime friend and classmate from Webster City, read some of my poems a few years ago at a gathering at the Kendall Young Library. He commented later, "I believe your poetry will be remembered long after your investigative reporting and books are forgotten." While none of us like to think of the time that a fifty-year career will be totally forgotten, I derive pleasure in musing that Bill Groves's judgment might be right.

ACKNOWLEDGMENTS

While there have been hundreds of people over a period of forty years who have in some way or another encouraged me to do this book of poetry, I would like to give special thanks to my wife, Jane, for her enthusiasm and for her suggestions and for prodding me to get the job done. Clara Bell Weatherman supplied editorial help at a crucial time. Others who have been particularly helpful and encouraging have been Bill and Jeanette Groves, Bart and Barbara Seney, Maurice and Mary Stark, and Mildred Sloane.

Kevin Lind, a skilled Iowa regional artist, stimulated me with his enthusiastic comments and illustrative sketches as the book started to take shape. Also, my thanks to Chris Bowring, an accomplished Virginia regional artist, who took on the chore of providing some of the illustrative sketches to meet the deadlines.

I would be remiss if I failed to mention the help of Richard Kinney, Director of Iowa State University Press, Chief Editor William Silag, Marilyn Keller and Jane Zaring of the editorial staff, and Production Manager and designer Robert Campbell. They made it better than it might have been.

Reflections on Farm, Family, and School

BALLAD TO AN IOWA FARMER

"Ballad to an Iowa Farmer" was written over a period of months in early 1989 as a tribute to my grandfather, Jim Clark, my boyhood hero and symbol of stability. Jim Clark could be counted upon to share his farm equipment or machinery and cheerfully to lend a hand to family or neighbors. Those who did business with him knew he was a man of his word. Grandpa Clark was never too busy to tell his grandchildren about the mysteries of machinery operation, crop rotation, or the care and feeding of livestock.

I was fortunate to have known that mustached and overall-clad farmer who was out of bed before dawn in summer and winter to take on the countless chores of farm work. For years, I had been trying to find the poetry form that would catch the admirable qualities of Jim Clark and other farmers I knew. The economic problems in the 1980s that crushed thousands of family farms caused me to take a nostalgic look at the days when an Iowa farmer with 160 acres of land provided a comfortable living for a large farm family. "Ballad" was a tribute not only to Jim Clark, but also to the thousands of farmers who broke the prairie sod and made the tilling of the family farm their life.

With calloused hands
Jim worked his farm
From dawn till day was through.

Within the barns,
Out in the fields,
He loved this work he knew.

Jim's weathered face,
His steady ways,
Showed pride in work well done—

3

His faith in God
And Iowa sod,
In summer rains and sun—

By free man's choice,
He worked the soil.
He wore no master's chains.

He plowed the black
And fertile fields,
Along the sweeping plains.

Jim watched the green
Fields turn to gold,
And hoped through harvest's toil

To see bins full
With corn and beans—
The gifts of God's best soil.

When neighbors helped
Farm neighbors out,
As farm folk often do,

In farmer's style,
Jim weighed each one,
And cut the trustless few.

With trust in friends,
No lust for power,
Jim kept his family first.

The wealth he earned
Was more than power,
For which so many thirst.

Jim won respect
From those he knew —
He was a trusted friend.

He did his work,
He kept his word,
His honor would not bend.

That family farm,
It was his life,
Hard work, but breathing free —

A fading thing
Of which we sing
In this nostalgic key.

That free farm life
To which we cling
In youthful memory.

THE OLD WORKHORSE

¶ "The Old Workhorse" was written in the late 1940s and rewritten and revised many times prior to publication in the *Des Moines Sunday Register* and the *Minneapolis Sunday Tribune* in the spring of 1957. The refinements for publication took place as I was reviewing Agriculture Department statistics on the number of horses in Iowa. In the 1920s and 1930s, nearly all Iowa farms were powered by workhorses, most of Percheron and Belgian stock. By the 1950s, the workhorse was a rarity, having been replaced by the tractors that took over during the manpower shortage of World War II. The few workhorses that remained were only the nostalgic reminders of an interesting past when teams of horses were often a pride-filled extension of the family.

A currycomb, an old check rein,
The curb bit for the bay —
The farm horse ghosts still linger there,
In shadows bare and gray.

The big black's hair is matted in
The brush upon the wall.
The mane hair of a young roan mare
Clings to the single stall.

The unused harness rots away,
And hames are turned to rust.
The empty manger gathers chaff.
The grain box fills with dust.

The double-trees and neck yoke lie
Unnoticed in the shed,
Except when curious children's hands
Stir memories of the dead.

The massive-bodied sorrels and roans
No longer fill the stalls.
The quiet is no longer pierced
With trumpet stallion calls.

Some stalls are rigged for feeding calves.
Pigs desecrate the box
Where broad-beamed Belgians stood and munched
With straw up to their hocks.

On down the road, five miles or so,
An old team walks the lane—
The remnants of the massive power
That plowed this rolling plain.

IN GHOSTLY STABLES

In the spring of 1989, on a visit to the old Clark farm, I walked through the barn and climbed the ladder to the hay-mow where I had played as a child and worked as a young man. "In Ghostly Stables" was written in its final form during a contemplative two hours seated in my car in the barnyard.

Empty stalls in ghostly stables
Where the massive Belgians fed.
Molding boards and rotting cables
Where the cattle made their bed.

Dusty troughs and sagging gables
In the ancient farrowing shed.
Vacant houses. Harvest tables
Now just visions in the head.

Farm with horses. Seems as fables
Of the farm youth life we led.
Ghostly stalls in empty stables
Bring back mem'ries of the dead.

HARVEST TIME INTERLUDE

In the 1970s, I made a brief visit to the farm home of Dale and Florence Hildreth, south of Rockwell City, Iowa. I shocked oats and ran a bundle rack on that farm for two summers when I was in my last years in high school. My visit was on a hot August day, but the living room was cool, reminding me of the deep pleasure I had found, as the Hildreths' hired farmhand, in getting out of the sun and resting momentarily in the shade of a loaded hayrack while awaiting my turn at the threshing machine. "Harvest Time Interlude" was written on the next day and was rewritten and refined in the months that followed.

The breezes of summer,
       that broke through the heat
Of harvest and August,
       were quiet and sweet.
A harvest time interlude
       snatched from my toil—
A moment of reverie
       next to the soil.

A moment of pleasure
       beneath my hayrack.
Ten minutes to treasure
       stretched out on my back.
An oat-bundle pillow,
       a breeze on my brow
That swings through the willow
       caressing each bow.

10

It ruffles the long weeds
    that grow by the fence,
And ripples the broad fields
    where green corn is dense.
It soothes and massages
    and helps me lose track
Of aches and the hot grime
    of loading the rack.

Too soon it is over—
    I'm back on the line.
My pitchfork is moving.
    the thresher belts whine;
I'm sweaty and dirty
    and straining my back,
And long for the interlude
    under the rack.

11

SUMMER STORM

¶ "Summer Storm" was written in the early 1980s at an airport in Ohio. A heavy rain had delayed my flight for more than an hour, and the rain on the windows and the solitude reminded me of resting in the haymow of a barn when a heavy rain was the only legitimate reason for stopping the exhausting summer farm work.

The couch was sweet alfalfa
near the haymow door—
A foot beyond the rain splash
on the hayloft floor.

The barnyard soil was gumbo
to the long farm lane,
And the raindrops beat staccato
on the roan mare's mane.

Beyond the eager rutting
of a young Hamp sire,
The cattle huddled hock deep
in the thick black mire.

But barnyard sounds were muted
in the rain's downpour,
And the barn became my island
in the storm's deep roar.

Afar, the ceaseless rolling of
the corn-green plain,
And, on the roof, the drumming
of incessant rain.

The loft was peaceful haven with
    its clean soft hay,
As I watched the falling torrents
    on that August day.

Apart, cut loose from troubled thoughts,
    a moment so secure.
The memory of that summer storm
    was destined to endure.

PRAIRIE PRIEST

Late in 1981, the women of St. Joseph's Catholic Church in Lohrville, Iowa, asked me if I would write an article on Father George Costello, a prairie priest born in 1857 who had organized the church in 1882 and served as its pastor until his death in 1938. The article was to be included in the centennial booklet being published by the church. I started to write in prose but decided in short order that this legendary figure could be dealt with better in poetry. In my childhood I had known Father Costello and had heard about his early days as a prairie priest from my mother, a member of his parish from her birth in 1898.

Father Costello was a constant presence at St. Joseph's School, which I attended, and I had served him as an altar boy for more than four years. I had been in awe of this stern figure, despite his gentle way with children. In my earliest years, I confused Father Costello's ruggedly handsome, gray-haired image with the God of the Bible and our prayer books. Writing "Prairie Priest" was a labor of love, as I pondered what I had experienced and what I had learned from others in those innocent years.

Through muddy roads
And summer heat,
Through snows that darkened day,
The Prairie Priest
With horse and rig
Went on his lonely way.

When creeks were full,
In summer drought,
And blizzard's bitter cold,
The Prairie Priest
His circuit went:
The youthful priest grew old.

Through countless births,
As oldsters passed,
When death was premature,
The aging priest
Was there with words
Both timeless and secure.

In later years
His voice grew harsh
In preaching to his flock;
From pulpit he
Flung bitter words
That stirred them to take stock.

He grew severe,
Perhaps too hard
With evils he perceived,
Perhaps too stern
With mortal men
That God's word be believed.

The ancient face
Was stern and lined,
A sadness filled his eyes,
But children brought
The kindness out
In gentle Gaelic sighs.

For children all
He saved his smiles
And kindly Irish way.
"Lo, lo," he'd grin
And pat small heads —
Then send them off to play.

As young folks do,
We saw in him
The image of our God—
The noble hand,
The great gray mane,
A Moses without rod.

For fifty years
He was our faith,
A symbol of our Lord—
A righteous man,
Of ancient face
That struck a God-like chord.

OLD BILL

In the summer of 1981, I visited an old friend, Bill Cava-
naugh, at a nursing home at Lake City, Iowa. It was the first
time I had seen him since his wife, Greta, had died. I had been
a close friend and admirer of Bill and Greta and their eight children
for many years.

Bill greeted me and my wife, Jane, with the enthusiasm of a
teenager and launched into comments and questions on contem-
porary national politics. Then as Greta's name came up, tears came
to his eyes and he said: "We were a team. With Greta gone the
pleasure's not the same. I'm ready now. I think it's time to go."

Tears welled up in my eyes, and I saw that Jane, too, was
blinking back tears. Later, as we left, she repeated Bill's lines as a
moving theme for a poem, and I jotted them down in my notebook.
It was the beginning of "Old Bill."

Bill's eyes welled up with tears at Greta's name.
"We were a team," he said to let us know
That life with Greta gone was not the same.
"I'm ready now. I think it's time to go."

His bright expressive eyes disguised his age.
His eager talk of politics was clear,
And yet Old Bill had reached the stage
When death's approach produced no trace of fear.

In ninety years Old Bill had seen it all,
From heartbreak to the most ecstatic joys.
A far-off war had cut down handsome Paul.
God spared the other seven, girls and boys.

Bill spoke each name with special father's pride,
And smiled deep satisfaction with his life.
Life had been good, though one of eight had died.
For he had shared it with a loving wife.

Through poverty and plenty they had worked,
From youthful romance through the trying years.
An optimistic Greta never shirked—
Was energetic through good times and tears.

Bill's eyes welled up again at Greta's name.
"We were a team," he said. His voice was low.
"With Greta gone the pleasure's not the same.
I'm ready now. I think it's time to go."

MOTHER

¶ In the 1950s, my widowed mother suffered the tragedy of seeing her fourteen-year-old son, Francis, stricken with polio. Within a few days, Francis went from a muscular 210-pound high school football player to a powerless stretcher case with no control of his body from the waist down. In seeing her rise to meet this massive challenge, I gained a new respect for her and a new appreciation for the strength she had been in my own life.

Woman of strength, from you, of you
    there came my being.
From you there came these ears to hear,
    these eyes for seeing.

And you have shaped me more as days went by.
I leaned upon your strength — no strength had I.

I leaned upon the strength of you —
Broad-bosomed strength, as young things do.

Your eyes were deep and gazed in mine,
And in those depths — admiring fine —

I found a hope, a power to see
The joy of life — what marvels be.

I found that fog and clouds and rain,
Compare with suns in what we gain.

You taught me music's soulful hope,
As much confused, with futile grope

For something firm, for something whole,
I found then music buoys the soul.

You taught my hand to work and play,
To do the tasks that come each day.

You taught my heart to love all man,
To find some good in each life's span.

You taught me joy in what's today,
To thrill in living, come what may.

You taught me prayers and dreaming too
You taught the best of what you knew.

And best of all and most worthwhile,
You've taught my lips to keep a smile.

TEACHER

In the late 1940s or early 1950s, I wrote the first verse and established the basic rhyme and rhythm for "Teacher." Over the following several years I refined it as I used it in connection with meetings of parent or teacher organizations. First published by the *Des Moines Sunday Register* in mid-May 1957, it was republished in various teachers' magazines and gained nationwide attention in 1982 when President Ronald Reagan used it in speeches and ceremonies with an education theme, including the Teacher in Space program and the National Teacher of the Year award ceremonies at the White House.

You are the molders of their dreams—
The gods who build or crush their young
    beliefs in right or wrong.
You are the spark that sets aflame a poet's hand,
Or lights the flame in some great singer's song.

You are the gods of young—the very young.
You are their idols, by profession set apart.
You are the guardians of a million dreams.
Your every smile or frown can heal or pierce a heart.

Yours are one hundred lives—one thousand lives.
Yours is the pride of loving them, the sorrow, too.
Your patient work, your touch, make you the god of hope
That fills their souls with dreams, and makes those dreams
    come true.

OUR SCHOOL

¶ One Friday in the spring of 1989, I received a call from Kevin Lind, a young Fort Dodge artist-musician, who wanted a poem to go along with a sketch he had made of his former high school, to be auctioned off at a fund-raiser that Saturday night. Within a few minutes after I left the telephone I had become enthusiastic about the thought of doing a poem that would catch the mood of the changing school scene in Iowa and across the entire Middle West.

I was not familiar with the Laurens school he had attended, but in several calls to Kevin I established that it was similar in structure to Lohrville High School, which I had attended and had visited in recent years for reunions. I rolled my ideas around for several hours before fastening on the pattern for "Our School." It was completed by midmorning on Saturday and dictated to Kevin before noon, in time for him to have it inscribed on the sketch. Poetry under pressure had worked because Kevin's feelings had meshed with my own on a theme with universal threads.

The biggest building in our little town—
The place from which we won the cap and gown.
Brick-solid place of structured work and play,
Of joy and laughter, sadness and dismay.

A worn and rambling special building now—
A monument to where we made our bow
Upon Life's stage. A testing place for youth—
A site to muse on poetry and truth.

The artless structure is a tangled maze
Of added rooms with style to suit each phase,
Yet filled with youthful memory—warm as gold—
Familiar as a story often told.

Nostalgic moments fill its rooms and walls,
And ghosts of friends still linger in its halls,
And will until its walls have tumbled down.
This school—the heart and soul of our small town.

RUPERT LATTURE

It was the warm smile and handshake of Rupert Latture that made me feel at home within weeks after I joined the faculty of tradition-laden Washington and Lee University in 1976. This wonderful friendly man had come to Washington and Lee as a student in 1912. He remained as a faculty member and, after his retirement, as a special assistant to President Robert Huntley. His ancient figure walking across the campus was as familiar and beloved as the distinctive white colonnade that graced the university campus.

Soft words enhance the outstretched hand,
    warm welcome lights his eyes.
His memory stretched for moments etched—
    recalling special ties.
A firm and loyal protector of traditions
    back to Lee,
And yet an open-minded man on concepts
    youth may see.
A steady kind demeanor to encompass
    those who strayed.
A man, a fine distinguished man—
    a timeless Colonnade.

MUSIC MAN

In January 1958, my younger brother, Clair, was discharged from the Navy and became band director at the little town of Edgewood, Iowa. Edgewood, in the northeast corner of Iowa on the line between Clayton and Delaware counties, had no particular distinction in athletics, scholastic achievement, or music. I stopped to see Clair and to watch his band rehearsals on several occasions. I was invited to give the high school commencement address in May 1959. By that time, Clair had been successful in developing his high school musicians to the point where they won distinction in Iowa state music competitions. One of my visits to Clair's band practice sessions stimulated me to write "Music Man." It was used by Meredith Willson on several occasions in speeches and was later published in the *Des Moines Sunday Register's* magazine section on March 17, 1971.

His face seemed stern, but warmness
    filled his voice.
It seemed to stretch to greet the
    youngsters there.
His eyes were quick in measuring each
    choice
Of woodwind, brass horn, string, bass
    drum, or snare.

A violin was held in loving
    grip,
While other hands plucked out a
    cello's tone.
A boy was fascinated by the
    slip
And slide of notes within the
    big trombone.

He looked beyond the fingers,
    short or long,
Beyond the lips so soft, and
    so untried,
To find the eyes with eagerness
    for song,
And willingness to take hard
    work in stride.

Uncertain fingers touched the
    slide trombone.
Self-conscious arms reached for the
    big bright bass.
Then unskilled lips brought forth
    a raucous tone,
And mirth and triumph filled
    the youngster's face.

A flute and drum joined in the
    ugly din
Of sound that filled the little
    practice hall.
No music this, though music was
    within
And waited only for his hand,
    his call.

A week, a month, a year from
    now he knew
That steady sweetness would
    emerge and hold.
Then firm-lipped tones would
    round and settle true,
And nimble fingers would become
    more bold.

These were the young with eagerness
    to learn,
To work, to blend, to follow
    in his plan.
And music's passion made his
    being burn
To be remembered as their
    Music Man.

FORTIETH CLASS REUNION

The fortieth class reunion of my Webster City High School graduating class was the first one in which ravages of age were apparent. I found it significant that success had taken a heavier toll on some members of the class, but surprisingly, some who had been content with less stressful careers had weathered time very well. The poem was written on the day after the reunion and was rewritten over a period of weeks.

With disregard for money
and for birth,
Adversity and age had
marked them all.
Nor had time — greatest
leveler on earth —
Been guided solely by
their rise or fall.

The lines of age were
etched within each face,
And gray was sprinkled in
their thinning hair.
But most had gained a noble
kind of grace
In facing challenges. They
had learned to care.

31

Most pretty girls flashed
    bits of youthful charms
That beamed through fuller
    contours in each smile,
Recalling the warm softness
    of their arms
In days when gentler touching
    could beguile.

The dead were not forgotten
    as we talked
Of days when games seemed
    vital to our school.
A gentle word of Burton
    as we walked,
And smiles for Krausey's
    daily games of pool.

War games and cars had cut
    their lives too soon,
And we could only guess
    what might have been—
Remembering each near
    forgotten tune,
And nights our heroes had
    the will to win.

But Jack was there, alive
    and filled with mirth,
And Gagey was more handsome
    than in youth.
While most of us had widened
    at the girth,
We'd learned to live and love
    despite that truth.

That teacher's escapades
　　were less a shock —
More in perspective as
　　the years rolled by.
And even those with morals
　　firm as rock
Admit to weakness, and
　　the urge to try.

The youthful lusting for
　　a curvesome blonde
Was on male lips in light
　　and mirthful way.
But triumph of survival
　　was the bond
That made us closer
　　that reunion day.

FIFTIETH CLASS REUNION

The fiftieth class reunion of my high school graduating class stimulated further development of the theme of our aging, but with a more light-hearted turn of phrase. The poem was written midway through the reunion weekend and was read and distributed to class members at the final dinner.

You squint your eyes
To scrutinize
The faces that you knew.
Then search your mind
And try to find
A lingering tell-tale clue.

A button nose
That can disclose
A fleeting memory.
A strange-shaped beak,
A special cheek,
Or voice that is a key.

A twinkling eye,
A breathless sigh,
A contour that's the same.

A knowing smile —
Flirtatious style
That gives away a name.

The fats are thins —
Time-ravaged skins
Confuse the searching eyes.
Slim jowls now sleek
Cloud eyes that seek
To pierce the grayed disguise.

Time-wrinkled eyes,
Age-thickened thighs,
Veil beauty that we knew.
But deep inside
Young hearts abide
And spirits leap anew.

GOING HOME

❡ My brother Keith died of lung cancer in February 1989, after an extended illness. He had lived in New York for forty years, but there had never been any doubt as to where he wanted to be buried. Keith made trips to Iowa every summer to visit friends and family, and always visited St. Joseph's Cemetery at Lohrville, where our parents are buried. In his last years, Keith always brought into the conversation something about the wonderful, free childhood we had enjoyed in a small rural town in Iowa.

The Cedar Creek was iced, the sky was gray,
When brother Keith came home, at last, to stay.
Light snow had filmed the creek and fields around.
It drifted slightly near the graveside mound.

The sharp wind swept in gusts. It froze the plains
Where we had walked in gentle summer rains —
Where we had run to swim in youthful play,
When make-believing filled each blissful day.

The frantic work to get the dishes done —
A price for extra moments in the sun.
We rode the horses down the country lanes,
And made believe that plows were fighter planes.

Much time we spent in playing cowboy games,
And fought to be the stars with famous names.
The memories warm, but now it is so cold.
And you are dead, and I am growing old.

Yet spring will come and grass will fill this knoll,
And creeks will thaw and mares will start to foal.
Then plows will turn the soil to soft black loam,
And Keith will be at peace, for he is home.

His last remains will rest in Iowa sod —
His soul entrusted to the hands of God.

A MOTHER'S FIRST CHRISTMAS ALONE

¶ My father died in June 1946 after an extended illness, and that Christmas was my mother's first without his enthusiastic, almost boyish help. Two of my younger brothers, Clair and Francis, were still at home, as was my younger sister, Mary Margaret. Conversations with my mother and thoughts of my father's eagerness and joy stimulated me to write "A Mother's First Christmas Alone."

The children are in bed and I must keep
The dream of Christmas that they learned from you.
I must put out the presents while they sleep,
In morning breathe excitement as you'd do.

You were so joyous, and with each gift
They'd find you'd act as if it were complete surprise.
Down on the floor you'd play with them or sing —
Act pleased though nearly all your gifts were ties.

I mustn't let them see that all's not right.
I must smile more, for I must smile for two.
It must be cheerful, as you'd make this night.
I wonder if they'll also think of you.

The presents are as gaily wrapped as then.
The tree's more lighted and at least as tall.
Yet here alone the quiet is so cold
It hardly seems like Christmas time at all.

THE UNINVITED

In the fall of 1946 or 1947, there was a birthday party at the home of a neighborhood child who was a daily playmate of my daughter Gjore. For some reason, Gjore was not included and sadly viewed the children arriving at the party a short distance down the street. I tried to catch that moment in a short poem.

Uninvited, sad, she stood across the street
And watched the party with a longing stare.
She heard a classmate's laughter, high and sweet,
And felt the long cold fingers of despair.

She did not sob out loud. But in her throat
There was a sob that lodged and hurt her more.
She said, "They prob'ly just forgot my note,"
But knew they saw her as they closed the door.

TOO SOON HE IS TOO OLD

In the late 1960s, I was reflecting upon the good time I had with my son, Raymond, when he was a small boy and regretted that I had not taken more time to enjoy him before he reached the more independent, more rambunctious teenage years.

Too little time to fix his toys,
And talk of farms, and cars, and planes;
And shape the dreams of little boys
Before the priceless childhood wanes.

Too little time to watch his face
Break into smiles at little things.
Too few hours to see him race
His playmates to his slide or swings.

Too few the times with him alone.
Too few the stories told.
Too short the time before he's grown.
Too soon a boy's too old.

REMEMBER ME

Nine months of lung cancer and its treatment had taken a heavy toll on my daughter Gjore's energy, but her spirits were up for Thanksgiving dinner in November 1989. Her energy was depleted, but the weight loss had slimmed her face in a manner that had restored much of the beauty of her twenties. Although we were both aware that her illness was probably terminal, there was essentially no discussion of her condition or the prospects of her death. She was absorbed in elaborate planning for a big Christmas party, and for family gifts for what could be her last Christmas.

Twice she alluded to her condition, the strong possibility of an early death. She had accepted the fact that she did not have long and commented that she hoped to make it through Christmas. At another point she reached over and touched my hand and said, "Remember me." "I will," I said and moved the conversation away from the subject. Gjore died on December 18, 1989—less than a week before Christmas.

You said, "Remember me." "I will," was my reply.
I said it with sincerity, not fully knowing why.
How could I know your preciousness would be in every
    breeze,
That I could find your selfless help in all that mortal sees.

The warmth of desert sunbeams, the gentleness of rain,
I feel your deep compassion in all that's sad or pain.
I find your love in ocean swells, and gulls that follow there,
The justice-seeking part of you—a base for every prayer.

You're the ripple of an oak leaf, the brilliance of a star.
The sky above in constancy—that's you where'er you are.
A song that swings, a musical, a firelight's glowing ember—
As long as there is earth or sky, I know I will remember.

BALLAD TO JOHN V. ATANASOFF

In 1988 my book was published on the invention and construction of the first electronic digital computer at Iowa State College by Dr. Atanasoff and a brilliant graduate student, Clifford E. Berry. It was based on a well-documented federal court ruling that the men who designed ENIAC at the University of Pennsylvania "had not themselves invented the electronic digital computer, but had derived the ideas from one John Vincent Atanasoff."

The federal court decision was made public in October 1973, but it was difficult to turn around historians who had spent thirty years accepting John Mauchly and Presper Eckert as the inventors. In the process of demonstrating to the Smithsonian Institution and the editors of the major encyclopedias that they should credit Dr. Atanasoff with the invention of the first electronic computer, I decided that the Atanasoff story was one that would lend itself to a ballad with a clear hero and a well-documented case of falsehood and deceit by Dr. Mauchly. I did not have to take any poetic license with the facts to complete my ballad to the "Forgotten Father of the Computer."

On November 13, 1990, President Bush awarded Dr. Atanasoff a Presidential Medal for Technology.

42

At Iowa State
in thirty-eight
John turned our world around.
With vacuum tubes,
he theorized,
Swift answers could be found

For problems that
had stumped the world
Of science and of math.
John reasoned that
a base of two
Could guide him on his path.

It started with
a long cold drive,
A drink, and quiet thought.
In darkened bar,
John found the theme
To solve what Babbage sought.

At Iowa State
in thirty-nine
His theories met the test
Of prototype,
then desk-sized frame —
A stimulating quest.

With Berry's help,
John built the rig
To test his theories out.
Then as a team
they built the frame
To banish any doubt.

43

The job was done
        when Mauchly came
To view the new machine.
Naive and proud,
        they told him all.
John saw no need to screen

What Mauchly saw—
        what Mauchly read.
This scholar was no knave.
This man of letters
        would not steal
Or soil the trust they gave.

Then John and Cliff
        turned to the work
Of science in the war—
No draft deferments
        to pursue
What could have mattered more.

John left the fate
        of patent work
In hands he thought were sure
To follow through
        in steady ways.
His right would then endure.

But Mauchly broke
        his trust with John
And built the ENIAC.
The plans derived
        from Cliff and John
Were clothed in secrets black.

And Mauchly took
    the bows for years
For concepts that he stole.
He dodged and weaved
    and outright lied
To hide John's rightful role.

For thirty years,
    he pushed his lies
For profit and for power.
In deposition,
    under oath,
Old Mauchly's "truths" turned sour.

In trials in court,
    the truth prevailed.
Judge Larson said it all:
John At-an-as-off
    was the man
Entitled to stand tall—

To take the bows
    for concepts great
Derived from his machine
Though ENIAC
    was steps beyond
What Mauchly's eyes had seen.

In U.S. court
    the record long
Proved that the concepts great
Were tested first
    by Cliff and John
In work at Iowa State.

At Iowa State
    in thirty-nine
John proved his right to fame.
The world around
    should know it's time
To celebrate his name.

Invention great —
    the century's best!
Genius too long forgot.
To right a wrong,
    we sing this song
To end deceitful rot.

Reflections on War

CAPRICIOUSNESS

The first version of "Capriciousness" was written during the war years as I was trying to catch the contradictory desires for adventure and security that burn within many young men and women. It was rewritten in 1959 after I suffered a broken neck in an automobile accident and hung between life and death for nearly a week. Knowledge of my precarious position made me more appreciative of the gift of simply living.

We love capriciousness.
Its whimsical and rapid changes,
Rearranges —
Makes life a moving book.

We thrill to vagary —
The wandering far and near,
Without a tear,
Without a backward look.

But life becomes futile
When erratic alterations
Leave it unstabled,
Uncabled —
When life has gone amiss.

The value of constant,
Steadfast things
Is realized,
And prized,
Across time's great abyss.

THE PROFESSOR

Dean Arthur A. Morrow was a short and pudgy law professor at Drake University in the early years of World War II. His efforts to hold our attention were often futile when pitted against the competition of war stories in the newspapers and the general atmosphere that gripped the campus and the country during the time.

Short,
Bespectacled,
Paunchy,
He was fighting a losing battle.

Lecturing,
Barking,
Scolding,
At students who thought it prattle.

Teaching,
Often
Preaching,
Trying to break the tension

Of war,
Of wings,
Of guns,
And deeds of valorous mention.

PARTING

¶ Leaving Iowa for the Naval Officers Training Camp at Platts-
burg, New York, had not had a significant impact upon me or
my family. However, this time I was leaving for San Diego,
California, with a specific assignment as a boat group officer on
APA 139 (an attack transport). The possibility of an assault landing
on a tropical island was chilling to contemplate, because the high
casualty rate of junior officers involved in such landings had been
dramatized in news stories and films on Tarawa and Iwo Jima.

I left my home today—a parting such
That I was dazed within its frigid clutch.
The fall with all its brilliance turning brown,
The sky, a heavy gray, looked sadly down.
And, knowing fear, without a real, full knowing,
A child was sad and fearful at my going.
A mother wept although my face was glad.
A father checked the tears he could have had.
I smiled, and hardly knowing what to say,
I tried to laugh their tears away.
My words were full of optimistic air,
"I'm lucky, Mom, and I'll take care."
But even in the speaking heartstrings froze—
Was I the first to smile and utter those?

You know you're not the first, nor yet the last,
And many brave boys felt death in the past.
Then though you smile, you know why mothers weep—
Why fathers clench their jaws and try to keep
A silence though a son may force a smile
And boast that he can walk unscathed that mile.

CLICKETY CLACK

The chill of parting with my family continued through the long ride to the Pacific Coast, and the sound of the train wheels on the track beat on my brain. I looked out the window at the moon and the land passing by, and I could not help but ask, Is this the last time that I will pass this way? Unable to sleep, I wrote to try to catch my feelings in the rhythm of train wheels.

There's a clickety clack 'neath the beam of the moon,
It's a clickety clack — a monotonous tune —
That seems to be saying I'm not coming back
As the miles speeding under me clickety clack.

As wheels are a-beatin' the rails in a rhyme,
It's clickety clack and I'm wanting more time.

It's cold and I'm lonesome — I'm leaving my home,
And the clickety clack takes me nearer the foam —
Takes me nearer the foam, to the ship, to the sea,
And the clickety clack is not waiting for me.

How I wish I could stop it. I'd like to go back
To the places I love, but it's clickety clack.

The rails and the wheels keep a-beatin' a song
And I'm leaving, I'm praying it won't be for long.
But I look out the window — it's dark down the track,
And the wheels keep repeating, "You're not coming back."

Then you try to forget it by hitting the sack,
But wake up while dreaming of clickety clack.

Then all the night long, you are going away.
You shudder and wish the return of the day.
You hope and you pray that you are coming back,
But the rails keep the drumbeat of clickety clack.

TOMMY

Lieutenant Thomas Kohlhaas was the younger brother of one of my closest friends. His death was a special blow because this young man had always exhibited such a sweet disposition.

Don't say a world moved, a nation rose on Tommy's death.
Just say he smiles no more and he is cold as winter's breath.
He is no more. Though he was youth, his story ends.
He did the thing he must for home and friends,
And that is all.

Don't say he gave his life, or sought the light of some ideal.
At twenty, men don't wish to give a thing so real.
Just say his life was snatched before its start
Because a world said, "Do your duty. Bare your heart."
And that is all.

Just say his warm, full, living hope is cold,
His brown-eyed eagerness will not enfold
The life they could. Just say he's gone —
Will never know a love-filled night — another dawn.
And that is all.

Don't prate of mock heroics. Only briefly say
He did the thing he had to do. He fought that day
To live. He lost a game he'd hoped to win
Because conventions say, "You fight or sin."
And that is all.

Don't say we're proud he died for this — our cause,
Or that there's compensation in applause
From fellow men. Just say we love him now as then
And pray youth won't be sacrificed again.
Let that be all.

IN CADENCE

¶ There was a good deal of marching in cadence at the Amphibious Base on Coronado Island near San Diego, and thoughts of my wife and home dominated my thinking. Mail was the only tangible link with the people and places I treasured more than ever.

It's one, two, three, and left and right,
And blue-green eyes in soft moonlight.

It's left flank march and right about —
I missed that step and there's no doubt.

And what's for supper? Will she write?
And one, two, three, and left and right.

Then damn, it's warm, the cadence wrong —
It seems we're marching awfully long.

Need liberty — this life's a bore.
And double rear and two, three, four.

Then blue-green eyes and hair of brown,
And don't let marching get you down.

And left and right and right about,
And one, two, three in cadence shout.

And skies above are blue and white,
In spite of steady left and right.

The trees are green and waving too —
And thoughts again return to you.

SMALL BOAT DRILL

As junior naval officers, we were expected to have some degree of competence in rowing small boats. Our first efforts to keep in stroke were a disaster, even with a skilled coxswain trying to keep us in time while straining to move the boat forward. After most of the officers had achieved a reasonable competence at staying in stroke, there was usually one who still had such a total lack of coordination that he could destroy the rhythm, and the coxswain would with disgust command us to "rest all oars."

With straining arms and flaying oars
    and little system to it,
They'd get in stroke at "Stand by oars,"
    and quickly they'd undo it.

The oarsmen dashed themselves with spray
    in pulling deep then light.
And bodies shivered in the cold—
    a rhythmless delight.

The patient coxswain, brown and hard,
    who knew his boats and men
Would "Rest all oars," stand by awhile,
    and start the stroke again.

And oars were fast and oars were slow
    but never steady going.
And whitened arms and backs strained hard
    in futile piecemeal rowing.

And smiles hid under lips that pressed
    in hard determined mask.
But smiles were wide when some smooth strokes
    were blended in the task.

BLUDGE PATTERSON

¶ Robert (Bludge) Patterson was my catcher when I pitched for the St. Thomas Aquinas Catholic Church softball team. He was killed in action in the Italian campaign while serving with Company E of the National Guard unit from Webster City, Iowa. It was one of the first units called up and became a part of the famous Red Bull Division.

You big and cheerful cuss — and kinda pudgy,
You didn't ask much in that letter, Bludgy.

You'd not complained because it was your lot
To spend the whole damned war in front-line rot.

"Like to get home and play some ball," your letter said.
And then we got the news that you were dead.

LIKE THE SEA

While anchored off the coast of a peaceful Pacific island in the staging areas, I found the constant ebb and flow of the sea to be a pleasant reminder of the quiet and satisfying life I had known in Iowa.

When the spell of being yours is over me,
It's the bursting, roaring music of the sea.

There's the swelling and encroaching of the tide,
Till it seems such power as this cannot subside.

Then the dimming, sudden dimming of the roar,
Till the waves lap only gently at the shore.

There's the murmured warm caressing of the sands,
And the gentleness of weakness in the hands

Where the warm, soft waves have lingered on earth's breast —
There memory clings of strength that's now at rest.

And the clinging and subsiding of the sea
Has a wavered ebbing clutching that's a plea

Till the sea's again the sea and land is land,
And the crest has left a stamp in soft moist sand.

Now the land has felt a touch it had not known,
And the sea took some of land to be its own.

DON SHELTON

Don Shelton was one of Webster City High School's most outstanding athletes—an All-State center his last two years when Webster City made the final four in the Iowa State Basketball Tournament, a star football player, and talented baseball pitcher with major league potential. I didn't play ball with him in high school, but did play against him in some pickup games after he was graduated. From a standpoint of natural athletic ability, I was not in his class. He was completely self-confident, as are so many natural athletes who seem to do everything right with little or no effort, destined to win at anything they try. Don was killed by a sniper in the Italian campaign as he stood up to hurl a hand grenade with his famed pitching arm.

Don dead? Must be some other guy.
That can't be right. Don couldn't die.
At least not yet—he's only twenty-five—
He's big and strong and made to be alive.

Don't mean he'll never die—but not just yet.
That body's never stopped for what it met.
That strength and will would not bow down
In front of any warring frown.

Death could not still that power he had,
That reckless air could not be sad,
And cold and still or crushed and warm.
His luck would keep him out of harm.

You say you're right that he's been killed?
That cocksure air and strength are stilled?
He's dead—dead? Are you sure he's dead?
That life has left him—he has bled?

Yes, war just took strong life in spring.
Yes, war can crush out anything.

PACIFIC SUNSET

 Standing watch on the bridge of a ship sailing to the west
presents a wonderful and colorful view of the full horizon at
sunset with its ever-changing patterns of cloud formations.

Clear blue aft, we travel west
Seeking sunsets where they're best.

Ship of blue, you dip your bow,
Ruffles white as on you plough.

Floral skies will silhouette
Youthful warriors tried not yet.

Ocean blue is rippled white
Where the bow has knifed her night.

Mystic dreams above the blue
Gold and red and sunset hue.

Red blend, blue blend, gray blend, white —
Fade into the dusk of night.

Starred blue aft — the colors fled.
Now the sun is in her bed.

BALLAD TO PRIVATE EDWIN LEMKE

I had known Ed Lemke in high school, but not well. No one really knew him, for he was a shy loner who lived on the eastern outskirts of Webster City. He seldom spoke first and acted a bit embarrassed when greeted. The biggest response was a hurried hello and a nod or smile. The boys he walked to school with told us he spent much of his time hunting small game along the Boone River near his home. They said he was a phenomenal shot with a rifle, and that he had a special talent at quietly stalking small game. However, no one expected much in the way of heroics from this shy and quiet young man when he went away with the Company E National Guard unit. It was a surprise to many of us to read that *Stars and Stripes* had hailed our Ed Lemke as "The Phantom of the Fifth Army," as "The One-Man Army" and "The Sergeant York of World War II."

When World War II was over he became a security guard at a meatpacking plant and later was a machine operator at a printing plant. I tried to get him to attend class reunions but usually failed. A book by another classmate, Homer Ankrum, on the Red Bull Division revived my interest in Ed's heroic exploits. A group of us decided to dedicate the fiftieth reunion of our 1938 high school graduating class to Ed, our unsung hero of World War II, and for the reunion I wrote "Ballad to Private Edwin Lemke."

In school Ed was
A silent lad
Who rarely said a word.
A nod or smile,
That was his style.
His voice was rarely heard.

Ed talked to few,
But those who knew

Said hunting was his game.
With stalking skill,
And gun to kill—
A young boy's quiet fame.

A pleasant youth—
A quiet man—
Ed learned his hunting lore
In days and nights
Along the Boone
In years before the war.

With Company E
Ed went away
To answer duty's call.
He voiced no view.
He made no boast.
He stood erect and tall.

Ed learned his job,
The weapons skills
And studied ways of war.
When friends were killed
He volunteered
For dangers some abhor.

Behind the lines
Of enemies
Ed found his time and place.
With stalking skills
And marksmanship
He found a Nazi base.

Ed cut their lines.
He shot them down.
Ed was a one-man gang.

Not once, not twice,
But countless times,
For Ed the praises rang.

His deed saved lives,
Brought victory near,
Avenged the friends who died.
His forays won
A legend place
For Ed—an Army's pride.

"A Sergeant York,"
The newsmen wrote,
In terms of World War One.
The legend York,
Ed's buddies said,
Had really been outdone.

Ed Lemke's deeds
Stretched over months.
He did it for their cause.
Time after time
Ed volunteered
Without the slightest pause.

A hero man—
Boone River man—
Whose hunting days are through.
A quiet man
We honor here
It's right—and overdue.

SMALL BOAT COXSWAIN

The coxswains were the "captains" of the 26 amphibious land-
ing crafts carried on APA 139, and they constantly supervised
the chores related to keeping the boats in near-perfect work-
ing order. They knew that their own lives, as well as the lives of the
Army or Marine personnel, would depend on their skill at operating
the boat and on the functioning of the amphibious boats if called
upon to make an assault landing.

Gotta clean your boat and paint it.
    Gotta stow your gear just so.
Lotta work, but pride's there, ain't it —
    For she'll take you where you'll go.

Keep those guns all greased and working —
    Won't be long before they're used.
Can't be fouled up — can't be shirking
    When the run to beach is cruised.

Not so big, but lotta power there,
    Though by ships she's like a toy.
But you're mighty in her bow there —
    You're her captain, Small Boat Boy.

TURNIN' TWO AND TURNIN' FIVE

Letters from home with pictures of Gjore, then just turning five, and Sue, then just turning two, led me to reflect on my good fortune in having had time with them.

Though a diplomatic jumble may present a hopeless view
With struggles of a world obscuring homelife's future hue —
Though the sky seems dark and clouded, and no sun
    is shining through,
There's a comfort in the thoughts of turnin' five and
    turnin' two.

Turnin' two laughs honest baby laughs. Soft smiles from
    turnin' five,
You know the sun's still high above — you're glad that you're
    alive.
Fortune may throw odds against you — block the things for
    which you strive,
But it cannot touch their love for you when turnin' two and
    five.
Years may mar their youthful realness, smiles may shield
    when they contrive,
But their smiles and words are only truth when turnin' two
    and five.

When a world seems badly shaken, and there's little
    seeming true,
There's a faith regained in seeing eyes so frank,
    so baby blue.
Though our meetings have been fleeting, and the hours
    are far too few,
There's much glowing just from knowing them
    when turnin' five and two.

ATTACK TRANSPORT

APA 139, like all attack transports of her class, carried twenty-four small landing boats for personnel and two slightly larger landing boats for tanks and other heavy equipment. In addition to the APA's crew, each ship of this class was equipped to carry between 1,500 and 2,000 troops and to land on beaches where no docking facilities were available. The APA was a sluggish ship with little firepower, compared with destroyers, cruisers, and battleships, and on them relatively little attention was paid to strict Navy regulations. But it was the ship that did the backbreaking work of taking the Army and Marine personnel and their equipment to shore to secure a beach.

Transport ship for the attack —
Boats she carries on her back.

Broad her beam and deep her power
Island conquests brought her hour.
Welded hulk of grayish blue,
Bottom flat — she's sluggish too.

Working ship all boomed and blocked,
Lines are straining — "regs" are mocked.
Crew in dungarees with grease
Got no time for whites or crease.

Man those booms, then scrub your boat,
Load, work hard, and then afloat.
Cargo—troops—fill every hold.
Fight power's slight, but spirit's bold.

Three decks deep in troops and stuff,
Going where the fighting's tough.
Small boat boy takes over there—
Leaves the ship without a care

For life or limb, and lands the men.
Mines and strafing—back again,
Boats all cracked up. Fix 'em now—
Land next time a-knowin' how.

Knowing how to pray to live
When our boat's become a sieve.
Knowing that there's fire ahead—
But for God and luck you're dead.

Mock that "battlewagon crease,"
Dirt-faced cox'n smeared with grease.
Transport built for the attack
Carries wars upon her back.

BROKEN SOLITUDE

On a sandy, brush-covered hill near San Diego, a young Marine and a Navy nurse lounged on a blanket, obviously enjoying each other's company. The setting was quiet until a bomber from a nearby air base roared overhead.

A blue-hazed mountain cut into the sky.
A sun beat down, and the grass turned brown to die.
There was a red-orange sandy earth around,
Except where green brush covered up the ground.

And now within a clearing there were two.
And all the rushing world was lost to view.
And all was peace in gentle talking there.
They smiled and laughed a bit—he thought her fair.

They talked of soft and tender things away.
Where they had lived and loved in younger day.
And then the air was filled with frightful roar
As planes droned in reality and war.

SUE

A letter from my wife relating the progress that our daughter Sue was making caused me to ponder what I was missing. I knew my feelings were essentially the same as most fathers away at war.

They've written you are walking now,
    and tell me how you play.
They say you've started talking in
    a baby sort of way.
They've written what you're eating
    and the funny things you do,
My mind can't help repeating
    that "you're grown up, Baby Sue."
How I'd like to see and hold you,
    like to hear you coo and play.
Like to sing you songs of sleepy time
    to close out every day.
Wonder if you'd gurgle "Daddy"
    as I'd hold you on my knee.
Like to kiss you, darling baby,
    like to hold you close to me.
Like to stop all this confusion,
    like to stop this senseless whirl.
Like to spend my night at home again
    and hold my baby girl.

BLUE PEACE

On dark and cloudy days at sea, the blue of the skyline blended into slightly darker blues of the sea and the varying blues and grays of the hulls of ships in convoy. This eerie scene often made it difficult to distinguish between reality and imagination.

It was as if we were a ship and all around was
    blue and sea.
And blue and vast was everything and all that lived
    was you and me.
'Twas blue the sky and blue the sea and grayish blue
    the fog between.
And blue the ship and blue the flame. You were the
    brightest flame I'd seen.
The blue of sky and sea and mist obscured life's things
    as death and birth.
And blue-hazed curtain in between obscured the gap
    from heaven to earth.

TO MY FIVE-YEAR-OLD

I was familiar with the personality and chatter of my preco-
cious daughter Gjore as a four-year-old, but the letters and a
photograph impressed me with the changes that were taking
place in her looks, her personality, and her talk.

It's been such a long time, darling,
    since I've seen your baby face,
That I hardly can remember how you
    filled your angel space.

Can't seem now to remember how you
    smiled or shook your head,
Or how your eyes would dance and spark —
    the funny things you said.

Or how you ran and played — or cried —
    the sunlight in your hair,
Or if you had an angel look, or
    only were quite fair.

But dreaming I can see you,
    though it's rather vague sometimes,
With the right lilt to your laughter and
    a baby voice that chimes.

And it seems I hear you chatter of your dolls,
    or triking fun.
I see the way your ribboned hair is
    dancing when you run.

When you sometimes ask me questions,
    I often have to smile
At the weighty deep, deep subjects and
    your curly-headed style.

And when I'm half contented that I've
    seen you as you are,
My dreaming stops. I realize I've missed
    the goal quite far.

The picture that I've painted is a
    four-year-old I knew,
And the girl I want is turning five —
    she's changed as children do.

NEWS TIME

When Army troops were aboard the attack transport, the news was read several times a day over the public address system. The soldiers crowded the ship's deck below the bridge with no apparent emotion but with an intensity resulting from their vital stake in the outcome of military engagements all over the world. Their expressions, as seen from the ship's bridge above, reminded me of cattle in the stockyards located in almost all small towns in Iowa and across the Middle West in the period before World War II.

Olive clad—immobile faces
Listen to the news of war.
At remote or island bases—
Cherish news and listen more.

Like a herd of penned-in cattle,
They can hope the slaughter's done.
Weigh each adjective of battle.
Cheer in silence each foot won.

Hope within and ever praying,
Though they are such earthy men,
Hope the blood bets they've been laying
Won't be put at stake again.

YOU'RE FREE AT SEA

The experience of going through the tremendous beating of several days in a Pacific typhoon on the welded hulk of APA 139 was a severe test for all aboard. There was unspoken fear that the ship would be broken apart, followed by great relief when the ordeal was over and we were cutting our way steadily through a smooth ocean.

Through the bridge and mast
The wind sweeps clean
And the bow dips deep
In the murky green.

The waves beat high
Till they spray the deck,
And the green salt drenches
Your face and neck.

Then you brace your feet
As she slips and rolls,
And the chow hall's
Littered with broken bowls.

But you don't look aft
For there is no track,
But a dream or two
Of the sea rolled back.

Oh, you're free at sea
Till the rolling thing
Has lashed your soul
To its steady swing.

LIBERTY

¶ Observation of the ship's crew coming back from liberty, whether in the Pacific islands or at ports in the United States, was pretty much the same. The details (real and imagined) of their drunken carousing dominated their discussions for days after we were out at sea.

It's liberty and time is off
and taverns fill to brimming.
And life is fast and loose and rough
and sailors seek the trimmings.
The liquor flows and women fall and
life is poured too fast.
Then drunken sailors totter back
to find their bunks at last.
And back aboard they hit the sack
with heads and bellies rolling.
They find a sleep — a fitful sleep —
is not at all consoling.

REFORMED

The consistent drunken debauchery of a substantial number of crew members frustrated the chaplain and in a few cases persisted in the face of the most severe disciplinary actions. A particularly distasteful incident at Legaspi made it impossible to avoid the conclusion that only the approach of death would bring repentance from a certain few.

Now a war is fraught with danger,
Whether Leatherneck or Ranger,
And a fellow sometimes stops a bit to think
Of how tragedy would follow
If the sea would up and swallow
Him or wash him on a beach to rot and stink.
And he may give up loose women
And his alcoholic swimmin'
And begin to hit the sack at half past eight.
He may stop all dissipating,
When he prays, "Lord, how's my rating?"
When he does you'll know damn well the hour is late.

BIRTH

¶ Dropping anchor in Leyte Bay near Tacloban gave us a close look at what the war had brought to the Philippines and to remote islands in the Pacific. Native villages were torn up or were tossed into near-total confusion by the encroachment of Caterpillar tractors and cranes and the construction gangs that were putting up storage buildings and airfields. The desire of the natives had little or no priority when balanced against the military's claimed needs. I wrote "Birth" after several days of observation.

Out of the churning whirl of dust,
Propellers flaying in yellow lust —
Borne on the ships and planes.

Here is the wide and yellowed strip,
Jungles lashed by a new world's whip —
Islands in labor pains.

Coconut groves — each green-topped stake,
Uprooted, battered. Wide roads we make —
Thrusting with "cats" and cranes.

Pushing the natives' village back,
Pushing the brown-skin from his shack —
Heed not if he complains.

Making his world the world of whites.
Futile is struggle. He never fights —
White has the power — white reigns.

83

Making his home a trading store,
Making his girl a brown-skinned whore—
Money for "love" leaves stains.

Making his child a begging thing.
"Money—more pesos," the infant sings.
Money becomes his chains.

Violence of action—tearing the womb
Out of the painted birth, out of the gloom—
New life as mother strains.

Giving him life that's more like ours,
Building his cities, building their towers—
Roads where he had but lanes.

Giving him good and giving him bad.
Giving him "happiness"—he'll get the sad.
Who can say if he gains?

THEY DREAM

My memories of tranquility center on moments in my boyhood in Lohrville when I was stretched out on the cool green lawn under an oak tree watching the sky. I am certain that many of the young men who died in bloody assaults on the hot and barren beaches of South Pacific islands had similar thoughts in their last hours.

A cool, green lawn, and overhead a tree,
And through its branches he could see
The sky.

In mucky hell of heat filled with debris,
They dream of home — what used to be —
And die.

ABOUT THE AUTHOR

Clark R. Mollenhoff (1921–1991), a Pulitzer Prize–winning reporter and author of eleven previous books, was a graduate of Drake University Law School. He received more than twenty-five major awards in forty-five years as an investigative reporter, author, and lecturer on fraud and corruption in government and in other American institutions.

He was a native Iowan, and for more than thirty-five years was on the staff of the Des Moines Register and Tribune Company as an investigative reporter and Washington correspondent. As Washington Bureau Chief for the *Des Moines Register* in 1973, Mr. Mollenhoff first became acquainted with, and fascinated by, the story of the invention of the world's first digital computer at Iowa State College, which he later documented in his award-winning book, *Atanasoff, Forgotten Father of the Computer.*

For the past thirteen years he was a professor of journalism at Washington and Lee University in Lexington, Virginia, and he continued to work as an investigative reporter in Washington, as an author, and as a legal consultant. *Ballad to an Iowa Farmer and Other Reflections* is his only book of poetry.